SPEECH

OF

HON. JOHN BELL, OF TENNESSEE,

ON

NON-INTERVENTION.

DELIVERED

IN THE SENATE OF THE UNITED STATES, APRIL 13, 1852.

WASHINGTON:
PRINTED AT THE CONGRESSIONAL GLOBE OFFICE.
1852.

NON-INTERVENTION.

The Non-Intervention Resolutions proposed by Mr. Clarke, being under consideration—

Mr. BELL said:

Mr. President: I cannot but feel some embarrassment in proceeding to address the Senate, after what has just transpired; and I regret exceedingly to find myself in a position which seems to require that I should speak on this subject at all, when so many measures of urgent interest and importance seem to demand the prompt attention of the Senate. Nevertheless, this day having been assigned for the consideration of the resolutions just announced from the Chair, with the indulgence of the Senate I beg leave to proceed.

Some question was made with regard to my views upon the resolutions offered by the honorable Senator from Rhode Island, [Mr. Clark.] I am not so vain, sir, as to suppose it of any public importance that I should state what those views are; but still I choose to avail myself of the courtesy usually extended to Senators on such occasions; and, moreover, to exercise the common privilege of Senators to express their views freely on any question, which they may deem of sufficient importance, and which may appear to be pertinent to the duties and powers of Congress.

I am aware, sir, that this subject has lost much of its freshness—still more of its attraction—by the discussion it has already received, and more particularly by the abatement of the excitement which existed in the country, previously to the introduction of the resolutions by the honorable Senator from Rhode Island. Still, I am of opinion that the subject has lost none of its intrinsic importance by the lapse of time, or by the consideration it has already received; nor, in my judgment, has it yet been discussed in all its more interesting connections and bearings; and it is for the purpose, chiefly, of expressing my views upon several aspects of the general question, which other gentlemen do not appear to have thought of sufficient interest to present, that I have risen to-day.

I wish it to be understood in the outset, that I do not propose to occupy the time allotted to me, on this occasion, by noticing particularly the arguments of gentlemen who have preceded me. I am aware that it might, perhaps, be expected of me to take some notice of the strictures of the honorable Senator from Louisiana, not now present, [Mr. Soule,] upon the course of the Administration in relation to the Cuban invasion, the officious intermeddling of the British Government in that affair, and the circumstances under which the Spanish consul returned to New Orleans. Sir, while I doubt not that the policy and proceedings of the Administration in relation to those transactions are susceptible of a very satisfactory explanation, yet I shall leave to others—who may be more familiar with all the circumstances of those transactions than I am, and to whom it may be both more convenient and agreeable—the task of elucidating, and of deducing from them the just vindication of the Executive.

I desire, further, to have it understood that I do not attach very much importance to the question so earnestly debated—after all that has transpired in relation to this subject—whether the resolutions offered by the honorable Senator from Rhode Island shall be adopted, if adopted at all, without amendment, or whether we may not incorporate with them some expression of the opinions entertained by the country of the intervention of Russia in the affairs of Hungary. While it gives me pleasure to acknowledge that no member of this body is more distinguished for his good sense, for his sound, practical, and statesmanlike views upon any question he chooses to investigate than the Senator from Rhode Island; and while I admit that his resolutions embrace every sentiment which I think important for this country to declare in connection with the Hungarian question; nevertheless, I mean to say, that I do not lay the same stress that others have done upon the question whether the resolutions shall pass in the shape in which they now stand, or whether they shall be so amended as to declare, in fitting and proper terms, the sentiment of the country upon the practical question of intervention in the case presented between Russia and Hungary. In my view of the subject, if Congress, entertaining the opinion that any important principle of international law has been violated by the intervention of Russia in the affairs of Hungary, should deem it expedient to express the concern with which the people of this country had witnessed that intervention, and even to protest and remonstrate against any future and similar violation of the law of nations, in temperate yet firm language, I do not consider that such a proceeding would disturb the amicable relations existing between the two countries. I hold that such a proceeding on the part of the United States would be no just cause of offense to any foreign power, nor any violation of national courtesy. Indeed, sir, there may be some danger that, in our caution to avoid one extreme, we may fall into the opposite one; for, while I agree that neither sound policy, nor a just regard for our own character and dignity, nor a due respect for any foreign nation with whom we desire to cultivate relations of amity and commerce, do not warrant or justify the employment of the language of invective, of menace, or bravado, in protesting or remonstrating against any actual or supposed aggression on their part, upon the rights of any other nation or people; yet there is a wide difference between such forbearance in language—between a firm and yet temperate expression of our opinions and sentiments, and the tameness and submissive acquiescence, which might be implied from absolute silence, when we conceive that there has been a violation of any great conservative principle of that system of international law, the boast of modern civilization, which has, by common consent, been adopted to secure the equal and independent rights of the weaker and smaller States, as well as of the stronger and more powerful, among the family of nations.

I have thrown out these suggestions rather to maintain the right of any one nation to take exception, by protest or remonstrance, to the acts or conduct of any other power, conceived to be an infraction of the law of nations, without being necessarily committed to any other or forcible intervention to compel its observance, than with any view to the exercise of the right on the present occasion. For myself, I am quite content with the resolutions as they were presented by the Senator from Rhode Island. If it were important, or proper, or expedient, to add to the resolutions, by declaring our sympathy with the fortunes of Hungary, or to protest against any future intervention by Russia in the affairs of that gallant people, I am not prepared to say that either the amendment offered by the Senator from Michigan, [Mr. Cass,] or by the Senator from New York, [Mr. Seward,] is in a form which could receive my assent. The language of the amendment offered by the Senator from New York I consider decidedly objectionable.

But I do not propose to examine the question whether there has been any violation of any great conservative principle of the law of nations by Russia—whether the interference of that power, upon the invitation of Austria, with the affairs of Hungary—a dependent kingdom of the Austrian empire—was such a violation; nor do I propose to go into the discussion of what may be the true interpretation of the law of nations, as to the question, how far one nation may be justified or allowed to interfere in the internal affairs of another, when its own safety or interest may seem to require such intervention. It is enough to say that, whatever may be the rule of international law, the practice of nations, as shown by all history, is—and, sir, it ever will be—that, whenever any great power considers that either its own safety, interest, or the success of its ambitious schemes suggests the policy of intervention in the affairs of other nations, it will not hesitate to interfere. It may be said with truth of the law of nations, as it has been said of municipal law, in certain conditions of society and government, that it is too often found to be a dead letter, when great criminals are to be brought to justice. It is a principle of international law that no nation has a right to wage war against another nation without just cause; and yet, more than nine tenths of the wars which have afflicted the world even in modern times, have had no other foundation, or pretext, than the lust of conquest, the love of glory, or of spoil.

It will be perceived, sir, from the tenor of these introductory remarks, that I have not risen to continue the discussion upon the subject of the policy of intervention or non-intervention by the United States in the affairs or quarrels of Europe. It is not a question of intervention or non-intervention, then, theoretical or practical; it is not the cause of bleeding Hungary, nor of her highly-gifted, though over-zealous and presumptuous chief, who no sooner set his foot upon our shores than he commenced to teach us the true interpretation of international law, and to give us lessons upon the moral duties of our position in the great family of nations; nor is it the cause of liberty in Europe, or of human rights in general; nor is it the question as to what is to be the fate of Europe, or the consequences of recent changes, or the present condition of affairs on that continent upon its future destiny—however interesting such questions or inquiries may be—that I avail myself of the privilege of addressing the Senate.

My purpose is to call the attention of the Senate, and of the country, so far as I may be able by my humble voice, to another question—to another and far different inquiry, suggested by the resolutions under consideration, and fairly embraced within their scope. That inquiry is, how are we to be affected—how is this continent to be affected—how is the New World to be affected by the recent changes and present condition of affairs in the Old World. How are American ideas and interests of government to be affected by European ideas and institutions. This I consider the great American question of the times; and one which may well occupy the thoughts and attention of the Senate and of the country. I could only desire that the inquiry had an abler expositor than I may hope to be. And I would that I had an opportunity of going into the subject under circumstances less embarrassing and more propitious and favorable to a hearing. I regret—I deplore—that I have neither the ability nor the favorable occasion for doing justice to a subject which appears to me to be one of the highest importance to the future condition and fortunes of this country.

I have said that the great American question of the day is, how is this country to be affected by the present condition of Europe.

What, then, is the present position and attitude of Europe in relation to the great principles and questions connected with the organic forms of government? Sir, I propose briefly to sketch the recent changes and, what I consider to be, the present condition of Europe in these important aspects.

You may remember, sir, that general tranquillity and confidence in the established order of things had reigned in Europe for a considerable period, when the sudden and unexpected overthrow of Louis Phillippe, followed in rapid succession by popular and insurrectionary movements in Italy and the German States, in Austria and Hungary, roused the world from its supineness. The simultaneous movement of the liberals in so many States, and their partial successes, inspired the lovers of freedom everywhere with hopes of the most beneficent results, and led to the greatest excitement; but the public mind, with the receding tide of republican successes, regained its composure without its confidence. The unsettled condition of affairs, and the power of contending factions in one great country still held the public mind in suspense, and all awaited the solution of French politics; perceiving, that upon that would depend, in no small degree, the future quiet of the Continent. That solution came like a clap of thunder to unexpecting ears, in the *coup d'etat* of the 2d of December. The excitement was now intense, and expectation was on tiptoe, until the question could be solved, which had no clue in the knowledge or conjectures of this country—whether the French people appealed to, as they were, with every external show of freedom of choice, would condemn or approve the daring usurpation of Louis Napoleon. While in this suspense, lo! tidings came that upwards of seven of the eight millions of adult male population of France had approved and sanctioned the decree which abolished the Republic; and confided to the arbitrary will of one man the power of reconstructing their Government. Thirty-six millions of freemen thus voluntarily surrendered their liberty, and gave their powerful sanction to the creed that popular sovereignty was not a safe element in the organic form of a government!

If the event of the 2d December was startling, these last tidings were absolutely astounding; and men's minds were set to work to account for the strange and unexpected result—scarcely yet doubting that the next arrival of a steamer from abroad would bring accounts of a spontaneous and successful uprising of the partisans of freedom in France which had hurled the daring usurper from power. But, astonishing as were the events I have just recounted, the fact—the most amazing to me at the time of all that have transpired since the expulsion of Louis Phillippe from his throne—remains yet to be stated. Contemporaneously with the first report of the event of the 2d of December which reached this country, came vague—and at the time little credited—assurances that the movement of Louis Napoleon would not only be successful, but that the peace of France, and of Europe, would be rather consolidated than disturbed by its success! And now, after four months—after more than a hundred days have passed, fresh assurances reach us from so many reliable sources to the same effect, that it would seem a species of madness any longer to resist absolute conviction on that point—assurances the more incredible from the first, when we consider that they were accompanied by advices that the King of Prussia, following the lead of France and Austria, was proceeding as fast as he durst to remodel the constitution of his Government upon a basis which excluded every vestige of republicanism.

What, then, sir, is now the recognized and well-understood position of the nations of Europe—the cradle, and still the great nursery of modern civilization—in regard to popular rights and free government? Let facts speak the answer. If what we hear be true of Prussia, then the four great Powers of the Continent are modeling their Governments upon the basis of absolutism—upon the theory that popular sovereignty, or popular control, to any extent in the affairs of government, directly or by representative assemblies, is incompatible with peace and order, and utterly subversive of the securities and blessings of civil society. Sir, a new order of things has arisen which decrees the abolition of the very symbols of liberty. Every monument of the transient existence of former Republics—every inscription, every memento of former freedom, is to be razed to its foundations—effaced and obliterated, so that no trace shall remain—no tradition be allowed to go down to posterity of the time when republican forms had found a foothold in Europe.

Thus, sir, the great and imposing fact stares us in the face that the continent of Europe has reverted to the old ideas of monarchy and absolutism! and liberty lies prostrate, discarded and dishonored.

And what, I repeat, is still more surprising, the opinion prevails, founded upon the most reliable sources of information—the entire mercantile class, the stock market, the great capitalists upon the London Exchange and the Paris Bourse, the money kings, who have their Argus eyes fixed upon every part of the Continent; and their secret agents in every cabinet—not only that republicanism is down, but that there will be no further commotion, no war; and that this state of things is permanent in Europe!

Can this be true, Mr. President? Can it be true that the spirit of liberty is extinct in Europe; or, if existing at all, so feeble, so exhausted, so dead, as to give no signs of future awakening; no promise of an early resurrection; and this, too, in the middle of the nineteenth century—and among the most civilized people of the earth! this, too, in the full and meridian blaze of science, moral and physical—in an age, which has been emphatically and universally proclaimed and recognized as the age of progress, to distinguish it from all antecedent ages and generations of the world! Why, sir, at such a time as this—in such an age as this—among a people so civilized, to affirm that a new order and condition of things has arisen which rejects and repudiates the idea of popular rights or sovereignty as incompatible with the ends of society; and that this state of things is permanent! to affirm that republicanism is *effete*—fast becoming an obsolete idea—that its merits have been weighed in the balance and found wanting; that the handwriting has appeared upon the wall, announcing confiscation and banishment to the partisans of freedom. Why, sir, I wonder that some gentlemen do not start from their seats in this Chamber, upon the announcement of so stupendous a fact upon any creditable authority—and yet the authority is the highest known in the range of human testimony!

And this is the advancing spirit of the age! This, the *denouement*—the final result of sixty years of revolution, of agony, and of blood! in the cause of liberty in Europe.

But can it be true, that the cause of republicanism is lost—is irretrievable in Europe? I have given you the testimony of the stock exchange and the mercantile classes. I will now give you, if possible, a still more reliable authority—the official and public declaration of the late Ministry of Great Britain, reaffirmed by the present. I refer to the declarations to be found in the late debate in the British Parliament, which arose upon the dismission of Lord Palmerston from the Ministry. The whole debate is pregnant and significant of European ideas and prospects upon the question of free institutions. But I will not detain the Senate by referring to any part of it, except the concluding sentence of Lord John Russell's speech—the public avowal of the facts and sentiments of which, by a Prime Minister of Great Britain, must be regarded, and will ever be regarded, as one of the most remarkable circumstances of the present century. I read from the London Times:

"I have the happiness to say that the relations of peace exist between this country and foreign nations in the highest degree. I trust they may continue to do so; and while I deplore events which have passed on the continent of Europe—events which I fear were but the too certain consequences of the Revolution of 1848—I do *trust* that by peace and civilization, by the intelligence which is daily pouring in on us, by the inventions made to improve the condition of mankind, liberty shall be at *length introduced* and established, and that, with religion, it shall govern the hearts of men, and produce happier days to mankind."

Thus has the knell of liberty in Europe been tolled; its obsequies publicly celebrated, and its fall wept! with what sincerity I do not pretend to say.

England—aye, sir, England! the proclaimed champion of freedom in Europe!—England, that sympathizes with the diffusion of constitutional governments on the Continent!—England, that has been so often depicted as the flaming sword which guards the eastern gate of the Eden of liberty!—England, acquiesces in the new order of things! What a commentary upon the announcements so frequent of late, of English sympathy with America and with freedom throughout the world!

The English Prime Minister, then, *trusts* that, by the increase of knowledge, by civilization, and the inventions of the age, liberty may at *length* be *introduced*—may appear upon the Continent, and bring happier days to mankind!

Let us pause here and speculate a moment upon this great fact, which marks the progress of civilization in the nineteenth century. Let us pause and consider the conclusion and the causes which have led to it, of the strange, eventful story, of a contest, which may be said to date further back than the first revolution in France—going back even to the middle of the fifteenth century, when the human mind awakened after a slumber of ages, to some conception of the civil as well of the religious rights of mankind. It is said that the last scene of the fifth and last act of the great drama of freedom in Europe is brought to a close. But I ask again, can it be true that the contest is over? I call to mind another fact in addition to all I have before stated in confirmation of the conclusion that all is over. A late number of the United Service Journal, a periodical of approved authority, states that the armies on the Continent number four millions of bayonets. And they are arrayed on the side of despotism. It is true, that some of the more ardent friends of liberty contend that the conclusion does not follow from this fact, that the contest for freedom is at an end. They allege that it has only yielded, for a time, to the overwhelming physical force brought to bear against it. But, on the other hand, it is strongly maintained that one of the results of the progress of the age is, that the bayonets of Europe have been taught to think; that they have come to regard themselves as a part of the people from among whom they are recruited, and that they will no longer be, as in former times, the blind instruments of their employers in making war upon popular rights. The idea, too, has been often proclaimed in tones of exulting confidence, that public opinion has become stronger than the bayonet. All this may be true, and is certainly very beautiful in theory; but from the complexion of recent transactions in Europe, it would unfortunately seem, that not only the thinking bayonets, but that public opinion also, has rejected popular intervention as an unsafe basis of government.

But a few years ago, it must be admitted that the current of republican ideas and aspirations was tending rapidly to undermine all the monarchical institutions of Europe. Now, all is reversed. Men's minds, perplexed and confounded by recent events, naturally go in search of some fact or theory which may account for the change. Some take the view, that there is no great principle or maxim, in morals or government, so fixed and established as to be free from the influence of fashion, the love of novelty, or beyond the reach of those changes in sentiment and opinion, which are observed to occur at intervals and periods of greater or less duration, according to circumstances, among mankind, even upon subjects the most interesting to their own happiness and welfare. Some bold speculators have gone so far as to affirm that all religious forms and creeds wear out by time, and pass away; that weariness and lassitude are inheritable qualities—that they descend from generation to generation, and that, in the lapse of ages, the human mind seeks, by a natural impulse, to throw off old ideas and sentiments upon all subjects of mere faith and speculation.

The theory is more plausible when applied to governments than to religion. The passion for civil liberty is common to all, except the governing classes, in any stage of civilization. The passion for personal freedom may be said to be universal. Yet how often has it happened, in the history of the world, that these passions have yielded to other and still stronger and more controlling influences? There have been periods in the history of Europe, especially in the ages which immediately succeeded the overthrow of the Roman power and civilization, and even in later times, when personal freedom afforded no security to life or property. It was in such distracted times that whole villages, and the rural population of whole districts and provinces voluntarily became the serfs and bondsmen to some powerful suzerain, or chief, who had the power to protect them from the general license and plunderings of the times. And so, sir, I can readily understand that a state, or condition of things, may arise in any country when, by the madness, the turbulence and violence of factions, the restraint and sanctions of law and government may become so relaxed that a whole people, however attached to the cause of free institutions, may seek repose and protection in the embraces of despotic power. So it has been, in times past, in many memorable instances, and so it is likely to be in the future.

The passion for civil liberty, strong and universal as it is, has been known again and again to yield to one that appears to be even stronger than that—the love of national glory. There is still another sentiment, common to the mass of mankind, that has had a powerful influence in human affairs, and one which, aside from religion, many regard as the strongest in the human heart—I mean the sentiment or spirit of loyalty to a chief, or the heirs of his name and renown. The servile worship of eminent men—of men who, by some sparkling or dazzling qualities, or achievements in military or civil affairs, have fixed the popular admiration—is kindred to it. If we would calculate the strength of this sentiment of loyalty we have only to consider the errors, the blunders, and sometimes even the *crimes*, which it often overlooks in a favorite. We, sir, can bear witness to the intensity and force with which this passion, or the kindred one, has operated in our own times and in our own country in those party conflicts which have become so fierce and formidable. Presuming upon the strength of this sentiment, a dictatorship is sometimes assumed in the direction of affairs, only less offensive and galling to the feelings of manly and independent freemen, than the actual usurpation of all the powers of government. I need not say—what every one at all read in history must know—that the public liberty has often been a victim to this passion.

But neither the love of novelty, nor the influence of fashion, nor the passion for national glory, nor the sentiment of loyalty, nor the servile worship of eminent men, nor any law of change, nor all together, are sufficient to account for the revolution that must have taken place in the opinions of people of Europe within the last few years, if what we have heard be true—that the arbitrary authority assumed by the Continental Powers is founded in public opinion. The revulsion in public sentiment—the reactionary feeling, must, indeed, have been strong and overwhelming, as in so short a time, not only to have reversed the rapid and fitful current of republican ideas, but the more steady, deep, and broad one which has been setting in so long in favor of constitutional monarchies.

There is—there must be still, some great fact behind. There must be some solution of this enigma—some latent or patent cause for a change so adverse to the hopes and anticipations which cheered the last moments of so many illustrious martyrs to the cause of freedom, within the last three-score years.

One great preliminary fact I assume as certain and unquestionable: It is, that what we, in this country, call the bone and sinews of society—the great and respectable class of industrious and thrifty agriculturists, artisans, tradesmen, shopmen, and the mercantile classes generally, have come to the conclusion that popular forms of government cannot be maintained on the continent of Europe, in sufficient force and authority, to accomplish the great ends of civil society, the repression of internal disorders, and the security of life and property. Whence this great change in the sentiment and opinions of the populations of Europe, after so long a period of conflict and suffering? There can be but one answer to this question—but one solution to this problem. It is, it must be, the ultraisms—the wild and visionary schemes and theories of society and government, of liberty, of universal equality, which have been avowed and taught by the great popular leaders of the revolutionary and republican movements on the continent of Europe, and the sanguinary excesses of many of their followers. These are the men, and these the doctrines, which have brought obloquy upon the very name of republicanism throughout Europe. They have enveloped a noble cause in a cloud of prejudice. They have frightened the timid by the exhibition, not of the horrid specter of anarchy, but the living demon! They have disgusted and alarmed the stout-hearted and more reflective advocates of free government; put arms into the hands of the enemies of freedom more formidable than bayonets, and sent despair into the hearts of all who were ablest to maintain its cause.

Let it not be said that the wild and fanciful theories of a few revolutionary leaders, and the excesses of some of the more reckless of their followers, cannot and ought not to be supposed to have had so great an influence upon the great body of sincere and republican patriots, in any country, as to seduce them from their principles, and to abandon a cause to which they had been so long attached! No. I agree that the dreams of the delirious disciples of any creed, or the excesses of the desperate and abandoned, who are always ready to avail themselves of any popular commotion to gratify their appetites for plunder or revenge, neither ought nor can be supposed to have had any great influence on the considerate and steady champions of a great reform; but, unfortunately, those wild and destructive theories of social and political reforms which have struck terror into the hearts of the liberals of Europe have not been confined to a few or to a small class of zealots. German philosophy, for a series of years, has combined with the popular literature of the day to ingraft upon the minds of their excitable and imaginative readers, all over the Continent, the same mischievous theories. New, strange, and bewildering theories of the destiny of man and of human society, and of the perfection of which both are, by nature, susceptible, have quite unsettled the faith and confidence of tens of thousands in all existing institutions, both social and political. The followers of the new philosophy, everywhere, seeing that their theories of universal happiness and equality are not likely to be realized in any of the known or existing forms of society or government, become the advocates for the abolition of both. Denying all imperfection in the nature of man, and seeing that the Christian religion stands in the way of their reforms, they are compelled to abandon their own cherished theories, or to renounce that also. And hence we observe that the policy of reconstructing imperial and arbitrary governments on the continent of Europe embraces the altar as well as the throne.

The great curse of Europe of the present day is, that the theories and doctrines of the champions and advocates of liberty and republicanism have, all along, proceeded upon the same error, which rendered all the philosophy of the schools of antiquity abortive, and, for the most part, utterly useless to mankind. They all proceed upon abstractions. All their theories of society and government—all their ideas of liberty and equality, and the forms they would institute to secure them, are founded upon some preconceived notion of what they conceive ought to be right and proper, without the slightest reference to any practical test—to anything that has been proved to be sound and practicable in the past history of the world. Sir, to get *right*, and to be able to construct true and practical systems of government, they must first reconstruct their system of philosophizing; they must reconstruct their own theories, and adapt them to human nature as they have seen it developed in the past—as they see it displayed at present. They must adapt them to the races of men, as they perceive them to exist, in all their varieties and differences of capacities and propensities, without troubling themselves about the question of original unity or equality. They must found their theories upon experience, and not upon fancy. They must come to understand that the competency of man for self-government is not a simple or universal truth; but that it is a complex and conditional proposition—that it may be true of one and the same people at one stage of their progress, and not at another; and as to races, they must come to learn that every race has a civilization peculiar to itself, and physical and mental faculties of various grades of capacity for improvement and development, as all history testifies. In short, they must adopt the method of reasoning and theorizing pointed out by the great founder of modern progress—Bacon. When they shall have done this, they will have taken the first step towards a true progress in the science of government. Discarding all unmeaning cant and catch terms about liberty and equality, they must come to know that there is a liberty—that there is an equality which is agreeable to nature—a liberty and an equality resting on a basis that will stand; and that all else is spurious, delusive, and mischievous.

I trust, sir, I may now be allowed, without taking my final leave of Europe, to pay a short visit to America. America—always open and exposed to every disease or contagion, moral and physical, that originates in a foreign atmosphere. We see it proclaimed through the columns of a thousand presses in this country, that the spirit of Democracy is necessarily progressive. I ask pardon; for I intended to divest myself, as far as possible, of every partisan view and feeling in delivering my sentiments on this great subject; but I am unable to proceed in my argument, without the use of terms and allusions which may seem to have a partisan cast. We are told that reform in this free country is a laggard; that it lingers far in the rear of the advancing spirit of the age. Sir, it is said through the same channels, and proclaimed to the people of this country, that too much of the old anti-democratic leaven still lurks and ferments in our constitutional forms and in our legislation. By a more circumscribed party, but still widely diffused over the country, and of no insignificant influence, our institutions are denounced as being oppressive and unjust to the natural rights of mankind, alien to liberty, upholding social forms and ideas, which admit of no equality of position or of happiness; that there is no true fraternity—no freedom such as the spirit of the age and the progress of civilization demand.

Whence this type of Democracy in this country? There can be no mistake as to its paternity. It is European born. It is the same spirit and type of Democracy which have undone the cause of liberty in Europe; and its mission in this country can never be accomplished but by the ruin of liberty in America. Does not every one know that the most popular and leading champions of the cause of Republicanism and Democracy in Europe regard with positive contempt, nay, that they turn away with disgust, at the very mention of American Republicanism? They scorn to receive our American, home-bred ideas of liberty. Why, say they, *You* have no philosophy; *you* have no true and lofty conceptions of the destiny of man, and of human society; you are far in the rear of European enlightenment upon all these subjects! Such are the arrogant pretensions of the European champions of liberty. Some of the more reckless among them have the hardihood to declare that our whole system is false; and that if it cannot be reformed they are prepared to destroy it; that it is a model which misleads the friends of freedom abroad; and that it had better be pulled down than upheld in error!

I should like, if I had time, to say a word about this age of progress. That it is an age of increased population, wealth, and power in this country, and of an increased knowledge and science everywhere, no one doubts. That is all for good. But I should like to know in what consists that progress of the age which is announced as the basis of reforms in regard to political institutions. The highest moral institution on earth, except religion, is that of government. What is the progress of the age in the science of government? It is an experimental science. New revelations of facts lay the ground-work for reforms and improvements in government. What is that progress in America? We have seen what modern progress has done in Europe in this department of science. But I ask, what progress has there been in America? Have any new and better forms of government been discovered?—any new principles brought out by experience better calculated to advance and secure the happiness of mankind, than the institutions as they were devised and digested by the architects of our revolutionary period? What new theories have been developed in the lapse of the last half century which show an advance in the science of government? Has our legislation become wiser and purer—founded in more patriotic ideas, and better calculated to advance the interests and happiness of the people? Are our public functionaries, executive, legislative, or judicial, of a higher order of intellect, of enlightenment, of patriotism, and of fidelity to their great trusts? Is there less of corruption, waste, profligacy, and favoritism in the public administration? And, to notice some of the ordinary tests, has crime diminished? Are frauds less prevalent in trade? Are life and property more secure? Is the administration of justice more pure, able, and impartial? Is the spirit of personal ambition less pestilent? Is the spirit of faction less turbulent and mischievous? And in regard to the great distinguishing characteristic of a people competent to self-government, and to uphold a Republic—loyalty to the law—is that more prevalent and abounding? But I cannot dwell longer upon this subject. I fear, sir, that this idea of progress is to be our ruin. Ninety-nine hundredths of those who talk of it, (not in this Chamber, of course,) and of those who proclaim it to the country, do not discriminate between change and progress. We are all progressive. There is a progress in time—a change in everything. We are not what we were. We cannot remain what we are. We must go forward. But a true progress in public morals and in society, which may justify material changes in American institutions, I wait the proofs of.

Mr. President, I have occupied more time in these general views than I intended. I must revert now to the main subject of inquiry; that is, How are we to be affected by the changes in the condition of Europe? If what I have said and what I have attempted to prove be true—if the present state of things in Europe is permanent—then let me say to you, what, in my judgment, will be the result. In that state of things, and under recent circumstances in this country, will be found the germ of a lasting hostility on the part of the Powers of that Continent against the Republic of the United States; and, sir, we shall see that the next great war which is to fill the world with its desolations will be a war between the Old Continent and the New—between the Old World and the New World—between the ideas, the principles, and the interests, and the passions of European or Eastern civilization, and the ideas, the principles, the interests, and the passions belonging to the new and more vigorous civilization of the continent of America. This is the natural order of progress in the civilization of the world. The jealousy of all Europe has been effectually roused and excited by the late and vast accession to our territory; foreshadowing in its results the profits and resources of the trade of the gorgeous East. As long as this Republic shall continue united and prosperous, it must continue to be a standing rebuke to despotic power. It will haunt the dreams of the enthroned masters of Europe like the ghosts of murdered princes, and they can never be at heart's ease until they shall have made one great and united effort to crush this disturber of their repose. Principles of Government so diverse—adverse interests, so deep and imperishable, cannot exist on continents between which the barrier of an ocean is removed by modern inventions, without bringing jealousies, rivalries, hatreds, and collisions, which, sooner or later, must result in war—fierce, protracted war—which can only be terminated but by the mutual exhaustion of the parties, or the final triumph of one over the other.

A voice whispers me, Where will England be in a contest between the despotic Powers of the Continent and this Republic? What guarantee have we that she would be disposed to interpose her broad shield between America and her assailants? Will kindred race and language be a guarantee of the friendship of England? Never, sir; as long as the story of the Revolution shall be handed down; never, while the brightest pages of our history shall still be those which record our triumphs over British valor and British domination. The dire and lasting hate engendered by family feuds is proverbial; and the lasting enmity of England is decreed by an inexorable law.

But may not kindred institutions be a guarantee of her alliance and protection? No, sir. The throne, the altar, the aristocracy, the whole governing race, including the wealthy middle classes of England, have as great a horror of republicanism, and of the leveling theories of the fierce democracy of the Continent as the Czar of Russia himself. Nothing can be more unmeaning, hollow, and deceitful, than what we hear so often announced, through some of our own journals, of the desire of Great Britain to draw more closely the bonds of amity between the two countries. Neither the cause of liberty, nor any interest in the diffusion of constitutional monarchies, has been the basis of British policy in this age, or in any other, in her relations with the Continent, or with America. These were not the causes of her involvment in the last general war of Europe. They were purely and simply the protection of her own interests and her own safety.

Will her trade—will her rich commercial connections with the United States—bind her to our cause against the Powers of the Continent? I still answer, unhesitatingly, No! If there is one great fact in the future history of the world that can be foretold with greater certainty than any other, it is the great conflict, not now, but soon to be, between Great Britain and the United States for the empire of the seas, and the command of the trade of the world. Instead of becoming our ally in a war with the despotic Powers of the Continent, Great Britain would have cause to exult; and let me say that she has at this moment cause to exult, and her far-seeing statesmen doubtless do exult, in the dawning of a state of things which may place all the Powers of the Continent, even Russia, heretofore in her policy friendly to the United States, in an attitude of lasting hostility and resentment to this Republic. Great Britain may see, in recent events on the Continent and in this country, causes equally new and unexpected, which may prolong her power and her ocean dominion to a date in the future far beyond all former hope or calculation. She would rejoice to see our commerce cut up, and our youthful energies paralyzed and crushed under the weight of a European combination. She may stand off, to be sure; but if the Powers on the Continent will only pursue a pacific policy towards her—if they will keep their ports and commercial marts open, on liberal terms, to her trade and manufactures, they will have her free consent to model their governments upon principles of the purest absolutism; they may extinguish every spark of liberty among their own subjects, and crumble into dust every republic on the globe. True, England may clamor for some concession to popular rights; she may write strong diplomatic notes; she will bluster in a thousand ways to delude and conciliate the liberals at home; but it will be all mere vapor; and the whole farce will be played off with a perfectly good understanding between her and her neighbors.

As I stated upon a former occasion, Great Britain, for the present, avails herself, as fully as she may, of all the advantages she can derive from the weak points of her cousins in America.

She has discovered that a little well-timed flattery goes a great way with them. She is now carrying on a courtship with them most satisfactory to herself. By a profession of the principle, and a practice of the semblance of free trade, together with some relaxation of her navigation laws, she has quite overcome the jealous prudery of America. In the mean time, compliments to the ingenuity and invention of Brother Jonathan in the manufacture of agricultural implements, and with ill-concealed chagrin, to his skill in the construction of sailing vessels, are showered in profusion.

I hope I appreciate as I ought the liberal and valuable features of British institutions; and above all do I appreciate the well-earned renown of Englishmen in every department of human effort—in the arts and sciences, and especially those which contribute most to advance the happiness of mankind exceeding all Grecian, all Roman fame. I must ever honor the land, as I ought, which has given to the world a Shakspeare, a Bacon, a Milton, a Hampden, a Newton, a Watt, an Arkwright, with a hundred other names illustrious for their genius and inventions; but, with all this, I regard the embrace of Great Britain as death to American development. Her approaches are like the serpent's, with honeyed and fair speeches on her tongue, but with venom and destruction in her heart. My blood boils within me when I perceive the signs of her successful enchantment; every little guileful compliment to American skill and enterprise carefully and ostentatiously heralded in the columns of the ablest public journals of the country, as though we could not feel assured, that we are entitled to respect, until it is yielded by Englishmen—as though the policy of England, artfully, yet systematically pursued, now as always, was not to undermine, and finally to pull down, the main pillar in the fabric of our power—the Union. No, sir, if it shall ever be our misfortune to be engaged in a struggle with the great Powers of continental Europe, we can have no reliance upon the friendship and support of Great Britain. In such a conflict, we must stand or fall, submit or conquer, contending single-handed—relying alone upon American valor and American resources.

I have now, Mr. President, closed what I proposed to say upon one branch of the important subject I have undertaken to discuss. I am aware that I have pursued a train of thought and argument which may not interest Senators greatly; but other and different aspects of the subject, remain to be noticed, and which I think of sufficient importance to claim the further indulgence of the Senate.

Notwithstanding the apparently overwhelming weight of authority upon which the opinion is founded, that the tranquillity of Europe will not be disturbed—at least for a long period—such is the singular complexity of affairs on that Continent—so many facts and circumstances exist leading to a contrary conclusion, that some doubt and apprehension may well be felt upon that point. If such apprehension may be entertained upon plausible grounds, none will deny that they deserve our serious consideration.

Nothing, I admit, can be more hazardous to him who would be thought far-seeing in affairs—which I do not pretend to be—than to predict, with any certainty of confidence, what will be the result, immediate or remote, of the present condition of the States of Europe, or of any change or events likely to occur in any of the more powerful among them. How utterly delusive, not to say worthless, all such speculations, even the most ingenious and profound, especially in relation to France, may prove to be, we have only to reflect that, at this moment, and while I am speaking on this subject, by the passing of a single breath of air—the going out of a single spark of life—the snapping of a single chord—the newly-invented machinery by which a great people are moved and governed, may be exploded; and the fires of a conflagration kindled which may envelop all Europe! Wonderful and mysterious Providence! that the destiny of a great nation—it may be of a whole continent—should be so intimately entwined with the fate—the life of one man; and he of no antecedent position, significance, or renown! Nothing can be more strikingly characteristic of the age in which we live than this single fact. It may well be regarded as ominous; and teach us that rationally, nothing in society or government can be regarded as so fixed and well established, as to defy convulsion and overthrow. The complication of causes has recently become so curious and intricate as to make all reasoning from them to effects abortive; because we can neither perceive nor comprehend the infinite variety of minute yet operative fibres and elements, of which the moral tissue is compounded. The faculties of the greatest intellects stand rebuked, mortified, and confounded by rapid, successive, and unexpected developments. Yet speculations and conjectures as to the future, however extravagant or visionary they may be, will still occupy the thoughts and imaginations of men.

The more sanguine believers in the increased knowledge and civilization of the age, as a sure guarantee of the advancing spirit of liberty, basing their calculations on the fact that the late changes in Europe are palpably retrogressive, affirm that the spirit of liberty on the continent of Europe is not extinguished; that it is only entangled for a time in the toils of the hunters, and that it will speedily break the vain fetters, and rouse itself to greater energies than it has ever yet displayed in combating its enemies. It is this class of speculators on the signs of the times who affirm that, at this moment, Europe is on the verge of the great war of opinion so often foretold—a conflict between antagonistic principles of government—the one supporting free, and the other, despotic forms.

There is another class who go still further in their conjectures, and suggest that Europe is probably upon the verge of a still more terrible and formidable war—a war between classes—a more sanguinary, destructive, and wide-wasting war than the world has ever seen—a war between the poverty-stricken masses on the one hand, and the proprietors by purchase or inheritance of the soil, and the depositaries and holders of all other descriptions of wealth, the accumulations of industrial pursuits in a period of a thousand years, on the other side. There have been wars of ambition and conquest, wars between races, wars of religious creeds, wars for civil and religious liberty, and for anything we can foresee, the blood of many more such wars may yet stain the earth. Nation will continue to rise up against nation, race against race, and the tide of victory will yet ebb and flow on many a battle-field, on which freedom shall contend against oppression. But there are several causes which will prevent or postpone for ages, either this last great, conflict which threatens the civilization of Europe foretold by some, or the solution of the problem propounded by others, who maintain that civilization, whenever it reaches a certain stage in any of the great divisions of the globe, among any of the races of mankind, must finally yield to the great law of change—to the inevitable destruction and decay, the seeds of which are planted in every form of society known in the history of the world. The civilization of any one race of people, like the nations they compose, and like individual man, it is said, has it ages, its culminating point, after which it must gradually decline, and be lost to view, or only live in history. But though the civilization of western Europe may have reached its culminating point—though its populations and the races of which they are composed may be verging to decline—and though in numbers overstocking the land, yet, just upon their eastern borders, there is still that great store-house of nations—of fresh and vigorous races, to replenish and reinvigorate their decaying energies—to preserve, to perpetuate, and it may be to advance their civilization. The discovery of this New World of ours, and the facilities supplied to immigration by modern inventions, will mitigate, if not remove, the great evil of redundant populations. And so I think there is no reason to apprehend the catastrophe of that war of classes, or of a declining civilization in Europe, which some of the desponding prophets of the times have suggested as certain or probable.

While I cannot give myself up to the belief that the cause of civil liberty in Europe is irretrievably lost; and while I am reluctant to come to the conclusion that there will be no immediate or early effort, by the more rational friends of freedom, spontaneous or concerted, to resist the arbitrary principles upon which the great Powers of the Continent are proceeding to model governments—to throw off the hateful incubus—to break the chains, ere they are riveted, which are forged to bind fast their liberties; yet I must confess that in the intelligence which reaches us from the other side of the Atlantic I see nothing to encourage the expectation of such a movement; and so I conclude that there will be no war on that ground.

But I come to a different conclusion from those who are of opinion, that the quiet which now reigns upon the continent of Europe is permanent; or that there will be no war within any short period. There are too many causes of discord; too many jealousies; too many rival interests; too many outcast, yet intriguing and influential dynasties; too many great armies ready to take the field, and, with all, the never-dying ambition and thirst for dynastic and national aggrandizement, to allow any strong faith in the hypothesis of continued peace.

In adopting this conclusion, I do not forget the opposing testimony borne by the stock market and the mercantile classes. Nor am I unmindful of the powerful influence of the purse-holders of Europe—the great moneyed capitalists—upon the questions of peace and war. Nor do I forget the plentiful professions of peaceful intentions by the governments most likely to disturb the peace; but I regard professions and diplomatic assurances of very little value. I look to more substantial facts I look especially to the political necessities which may drive a great nation to war. Notwithstanding all the assurances we receive from abroad of permanent tranquillity, that there still exists some uneasiness in Europe on that subject, we have only to recur to the fact that all the States of that continent are looking carefully to the condition of their national defenses; and while they all profess a willingness to disarm, they are increasing their armaments, both by sea and land. In addition to this, when we consider that there are now four millions of bayonets ready to be put in motion; and that the different maritime powers can put afloat two thousand ships-of-war, who shall say that there is no ground to apprehend a war in Europe?

I am aware that there are many causes existing in great force in Europe to make peace desirable. The enormous public debt, exceeding in the aggregate $7,000,000,000, under which the States of Europe are weighed down, may restrain the temptations to war, as it would undoubtedly cripple their military energies; but this is an argument which, like a two-edged weapon, cuts both ways. To pay the interest on this debt, and sustain public credit, takes the bread from the mouth of labor, engenders discontent among the thrifty and industrious classes, and desperation among the impoverished. Besides, four millions of armed soldiery, though their swords are unsheathed, must be fed and paid; hence the constant temptation to try the chances of war, and by forced contributions to throw upon their neighbors the burden of their support. The only remedy for this state of things is a general disarming by the great Powers, which their mutual jealousies will not permit.

There is a more potent influence still, that may possibly exist, to restain the Governments of Europe, and compel them to keep peace. The republican ideas and fierce democratic spirit which have so deeply infected their populations of late, and which has been the key to their policy for the last four years, may yet exist in sufficient force to control their councils. The snake that crept into the palaces of kings, may be scotched—not killed. The popular volcano that burst forth in 1848 with such fury, may not be burnt out; it may only slumber; and the vibratory motions of the mountain may impart fears of another irruption and outporing of the burning lava. If this should be so, all causes of discord, all mutual jealousies, all ambitious schemes will be suspended, until this common danger to the internal peace of the States of Europe shall pass away, or cease to be formidable. But I have thrown out these suggestions, upon an assumption which I see little reason to justify. The danger of popular commotions appears already to have passed, and I recur to the opinion already expressed, that the promise of a continued peace will not be realized.

France holds in her hands the issue of peace or of war. If she is quiet, all may be quiet. But can she—will she be quiet? She cannot. Louis Napoleon must disturb the peace of Europe or fall. It is upon France that the world now fixes its gaze; and with whatever seeming composure the result of her present anomalous position, and the development of her policy may be awaited, it is impossible but that the most callous and fearless statesman of the times must expect them with some solicitude. It is true, this second Napoleon may be suddenly cut off. It is true there may be a revulsion of public sentiment so universal as to drive him from power. In either of these events France may become once more the prey of faction; and relieve the apprehensions of her neighbors, and of all Europe, by exhausting her energies and resources, in rending her own vitals. But if Louis Napoleon shall survive the perils which attend him in the initiative operations of his government, then, I say, France will become aggressive. If there was nothing in the singular spirit, and, to me, mystical genius of that daring man, who has seized into his own hands the construction of a government for a great people, leading to the conclusion that he would become aggressive, and plunge his country into war, he is still under a political necessity to make war. It is true that in doing so he may but rush upon his fate. Be it so. He cannot pause in his career. He must give employment to his four hundred thousand soldiers, or they will divide and assimilate with the factions, or fraternize with the republicans. At all events, to prevent these dissensions in his army, he must have the control of large means; and they can only be acquired by levying contributions upon the resources of his neighbors. He wants, too, the prestige of military renown to still further conciliate and consolidate the esteem and affections of Frenchmen.

This remarkable man has hitherto in his policy, his tact and energy in civil affairs, evinced many kindred qualities, and trod with striking fidelity in the footsteps of his illustrious relative. Doubtless, like him, he considers himself the child of destiny—born to carry out all that was projected by the great Napoleon: Imperial power attained—the boundaries of France enlarged to the Rhine—the kingdom of Italy reconstructed and restored—the pride of England humbled, or her power broken, and a barrier interposed to the ambition of Russia, or a close league with that great Power for an equal partition of the empire of the world!

The great Julius fell by the daggers of domestic conspirators; and his nephew, Octavius, a stripling, unknown to fame, after a sanguinary struggle with the leaders of opposing factions, with the aid of the distractions of the times and an adroit coalition with Antony, succeeded to the power of his illustrious uncle. The great Napoleon fell by a combination of all Europe against him; and his nephew, Louis Napoleon, after a longer interval of changing dynasties and contending factions, has succeeded to his power; a man who seems to combine all those qualities of a profound dissimulation and strategy in civil affairs, with the additional advantage of personal courage, which enabled his prototype, Octavius, to succeed, in what was, at first, regarded a desperate and hopeless enterprise. In all history can there be found so many striking coincidences in the leading features, incidents, and fortunes of two great families—in the circumstances of two great political revolutions; one of which changed the condition and destiny of ancient civilization, and the other, it may be, is destined to change that of modern Europe. The parallel fails in the persons of Nicholas and Antony. Nicholas is a very different personage from the pleasure-loving Antony; but still he may not disdain an alliance with the only Power that can curb his ambition in the west of Europe, and he may choose to share equally, if he cannot win universal dominion. On the continent of Europe there are now, in truth, but two great Powers—France and Russia—or at most three, if Prussia be so considered. Austria lies prostrate and paralyzed by the variety and implacable antipathies of the races which occupy her provinces and dependencies. Prussia must be more or less fettered by the jealousies of the petty sovereignties in her neighborhood, and the democratic spirit which may still infect her subjects; but the great German nationality, including Prussia, may be conciliated by a tripartite partition. The provinces of the lower Danube, and all Turkey, with the prospect of further acquisitions in Asia, may suffice Russia. England may be intimidated, or her power broken, by reviving the continental policy of the great Napoleon.

But I have not time to pursue these speculations, as to all the various combinations that may arise out of a state of war, or their consequences.

If I am asked, why I give such prominence to France in holding the issues of peace and war—is she so powerful; is she so formidable; or will she have the audacity, under present circumstances, to disturb the peace of Europe?—I answer, that France, united under a favorite chief, has not only the courage to commence a war, but the power to become formidable to her neighbors. She is formidable not only from her thirty-six millions of inhabitants, and her compact territory, but from the gallant, excitable, and glory-loving character of her population; the French being now, as they have always been, the most warlike race of Europe—perhaps of the world. Twice has France, in the earlier periods of her history, rolled back the tide of conquest which threatened to change the destiny of Europe; twice has she, single-handed, protected its religion and its civilization—once on the plains of Chalons, where she met and overthrew Attila, and his host of three hundred thousand warriors collected from the hordes of Asia; a second time under the lead of the famous Charles Martell, when she checked the victorious career of the Moslem power, in the neighborhood of Tours. Twice has she been upon the point of subjecting all Europe to her dominion—once under Louis the Fourteenth; and, again, at a period so recent that it seems only of yesterday, under the auspices of the great Napoleon. Twice, in her career, has she succumbed; and then only when a world rose in arms against her. Such is France.

If Louis Napoleon has the sagacity and the ambition which I attribute to him, he will neglect no expedient to still further attach the French people to his fortunes. The French have become essentially democratic in their spirit and feeling; that tendency must be counteracted by counter influences. That spirit, strong as it is, has yet, again and again, yielded to a stronger passion—the love of national glory. Under the intoxication of that passion, twice have the French people surrendered their liberties; and there will not be wanting stimulants or occasions to rouse and keep alive that passion. The pride of all true Frenchmen was humbled on the field of Waterloo. That wound to her national vanity remains to be soothed or avenged. Louis Napoleon may bide his time for that; he may find some more feasible undertaking in which to flesh his maiden sword. If he does not find it among his neighbors, he may look to another continent. Africa presents too barren a field for splendid achievements. He may even be tempted to cast his eyes upon America. The recollection of the haughty and dictatorial menace yielded to by Louis Philippe, under which the last installment of the French indemnity was paid, still rankles in the bosoms of Frenchmen; but I beg pardon. I know how wild the idea will be considered; but I think it is not extravagant to suppose that, backed by jealousies and resentments of the other Continental Powers towards the United States, Louis Napoleon, perceiving the defenseless condition of our extended ocean frontier, and counting on his superior naval force, may seek to win renown by seizing and laying under contributions our rich and flourishing cities upon the Atlantic coast. Nay, he may be tempted still further, and seek to indemnify France for the loss of empire in America, in the cession of Louisiana, by attempting the permanent conquest of the Pacific coast. I repeat, that I am aware that this may be regarded as an extravagant and irrational conjecture; but who, at this day, and after all the wonders of the times, will say that it is incredible? But I must cease these speculations upon this prolific subject.

Senators may inquire, to what practical conclusion I design to apply all that I have said upon this branch of the subject? In the first place, if, upon a review of the whole ground, the position I have assumed, that at no distant day—in six months, in twelve, or at most in twenty-four months—a war will be kindled in Europe upon some pretext, or of some character or other, be well founded, then I undertake to predict that the United States will sooner or later, be drawn within its vortex; and, if this hypothesis shall seem to be supported by plausible reasons, then a further practical inquiry will be, what should we do to be prepared to meet the exigency?

In some of the views presented in the course of my remarks, it will be recollected that I supposed a state of things might exist in Europe which would leave the United States no option as to the question of peace or war—a state of things, which would lead to a hostile combination of all the despotic Powers of the Continent against the Republic of America. That may never happen.

But should that war of opinion, so long predicted—that war of principle—that great conflict between the free and the despotic forms of government—should such a war as that arise in Europe, do you think, Mr. President, as a sound practical statesman, and after your experience and observation of this country, and its present population—do you suppose that if such a conflict should arise in Europe—a conflict involving the settlement of principles which may have universal ascendency for centuries—that we should be so unimpressible, so indifferent, that we could not be drawn into it, despite all calculations of policy or of interest? Do you conceive, sir, with your knowledge of the heart of this country at this day, that a cold and sordid calculation of mercantile profit—that the devotion to Mammon, or any more laudable service, would be so faithful and intense, as to restrain even those reckless passions and emotions which belong to our nature, to say nothing of freezing up all generous and noble impulses, tempting us to enlist on the side of freedom, in such a strife? No; the time has never been, when, in any one country in Christendom, mind meets mind in fierce conflict upon principles which touch nearly the social feelings and interests of men, the mental strife, would not become contagious and move the sympathies of every other. But let the clash of arms add to the excitement, and the blood will be stirred and fired in its inmost recesses. Let the tidings of such a conflict—such a war of opinion, but reach our shores, and, my word for it, whatever may be the conclusions of mere policy, Young and Old America alike, will be swayed to and fro by the passions natural to the occasion, like the trees of a forest swept by a strong wind. Little time, I ween, would be allowed for weighing the counsels of the illustrious and immortal sages of fifty years ago. Nor are the feelings and calculations which sway the twenty millions of freemen of this day, the same which controlled the two or three millions of fifty years ago. All change is not progress; but the law of change, under changing circumstances and conditions, is inexorable. We have our destined career to run. Time progresses; so do nations. They cannot stand still, until the time of maturity and manhood is passed; as yet we go forward; and we will go forward; whether for good, is another question. We may not, however, be put to the test of a war of opinion in Europe, at this juncture.

But if a war should spring up in Europe of the old-fashioned kind—a war of aggression on one side, and defense on the other—a war of ambition and conquest—with the feelings of jealousy and of resentment which may exist on the part of the nations of Europe against the United States at this time—do you suppose that a war can rage in Europe for one year—especially if any of the great maritime Powers be parties to it, without compromising the peace of this country? Our commerce and navigation are too extensive and widely diffused; the general competition for the trade of the world is become too fierce to allow any escape from a collision with the belligerents of Europe. Have you not seen, sir, in the last few years, how difficult it is, even in times of peace, to digest the insults which the war-vessels of Great Britain, presuming upon their superior naval power, occasionally offer to our flag? But let there once be war, and you will soon perceive the difference in the calculations and feelings which control the people of this country, and of this generation, and those which controlled them fifty years ago. Since that period, we have grown six or seven-fold greater in population and resources; and, true to the characteristic traits of our lineage, we have grown in conceit of our puissance still more. Neither our temper, nor our prudence improves with the changing circumstances of our condition and resources. Let there be a war in Europe, and the first open violation of our neutral rights—the first breach of the accustomed courtesies to our flag, will be instantly retaliated, and thus the war would be begun; all unprepared as we may be. And let me say to the people of this country that, with the feelings which exist probably at this moment in Europe, any of the considerable maritime Powers of that continent would be nothing loth to accept the issue of war thus presented. The weak points in our condition—our six thousand miles of inadequately protected sea-coast, to say nothing of other causes which may paralyze our energies—are as well understood abroad as at home. And let me say further, under existing circumstances, that it will be rare good fortune if, in any European war in which we shall be engaged, we shall not have the sympathies of every other Power of that continent enlisted against us, except only such as may be strengthened by our interposition.

Before I conclude, it may be well to turn for a moment to those evidences of that sober discretion—that steady adherence to home interests—that reverence for the teachings of our ancestors—that conciliatory and forbearing spirit towards foreign Powers, so much relied upon, to shield us from the wasting and ruinous folly of foreign wars, exhibited in the last few years.

It is true that in the matter of the Cuban invasion, the intervention of England, and the return of the Spanish consul to New Orleans, our Government has pursued a policy singularly modest, as respects any conceit of our own pretensions, and in the highest degree forbearing and conformable to a peace policy.

But let us see whether we have manifested equal discretion and forbearance, and an equally conciliatory spirit in regard to the recent disorders on the continent of Europe.

It was but natural that our sympathies should be deeply moved by the gallant struggle of the Hungarians in their attempt to maintain their nationality, and to assert their liberty and independence. It was but just and natural that when the Austrian oppressors were driven out of Hungary, and trembled on the verge of defeat under the walls of Vienna, we should have beheld with no little indignation the intervention of the Czar of Russia in arresting the victorious career of Hungary. Nor was it possible that we should not be deeply moved by the atrocious cruelties alleged to have been—and, as we suppose, were—perpetrated by Austria against the captive Hungarian chiefs. Nor was it to be supposed that the popular feeling would not find expression through public journals, public meetings, and various other channels of communication to the world. Nor could it have been supposed, under such circumstances, that, through the same *media*, the popular ideas and theories of governments and human rights in general, should not be manifested in violent invectives and denunciations against the despotic principles and policy of the Austrian and Russian Governments. All that might have been expected, and could not have been a ground of complaint.

But these expressions of popular feelings and principles did not stop there. One of the most distinguished and eminent statesmen of the country—and I refer to this in no personal unkindness to the honorable Senator, [Mr. Cass]—brought forward a resolution to suspend all diplomatic intercourse with one of those Powers, (Austria.) And afterwards, another Senator, who has attained considerable distinction in the country, moved a resolution, which was acceded to by the Senate, calling upon the President to interpose his good offices for the release of Kossuth, and his companions in exile, from their captivity in Turkey, and to tender to him a national vessel to bear him and his suite to America. Kossuth and his companions were accordingly released, and ostentatiously borne, under the national flag, to our shores, where he was received with triumphal honors. But this did not suffice. After we had thus, and to this extent, interfered in the affairs and quarrels of two of the great Powers of Europe, we proceeded still further to provoke them by a breach of national courtesy—such a breach as is never forgotten or forgiven, however the revenge may be delayed. The man, already so highly honored, was at the time, and is now, regarded by the Emperor of Austria the prime mover—the living, animating principle of an internal convulsion which shook his throne to its foundation—brought humiliation upon his House—attached a stain to the proud escutcheon of the Cæsars, that can never be effaced; the man who seeks to be to the Czar of Russia what Sir Sidney Smith sought to be to Napoleon, his evil genius—dedicating his life, his genius, and his eloquence, to the disparagement of his character—preaching a crusade against his policy, his power, and the principles of his government—the man, who at the same time is proclaimed to be, at once, the martyr and the apostle of liberty in Europe—this man, by a vote of the Senate—their attention being called to him in a message of the President of the United States himself—was invited to the seat of the National Government, entertained at the public expense, and by a formal reception in open session of the Senate, had honors heaped upon him which the proudest citizen of the ancient Commonwealth of Rome might not have declined. A greater insult to those two great monarchies, Russia and Austria, you could not have inflicted by an open declaration of war. How idle, how ridiculous, after this, to be gravely debating and considering whether we shall proceed to express our sympathy with the fortunes of Hungary, or to protest against the intervention of Russia in her affairs, by further resolutions; or as to what shall be their forms; unless, indeed, we desire still further to provoke and insult Russia and Austria, by a more formal declaration of our implacable hatred of them.

Now, sir, from these proceedings we may form some estimate of the true character and extent of that moderation and sober discretion of the American people and of their representatives, of the present times and generation, so confidently relied upon to keep us in the faith and in the counsels of the fathers of the Republic. Truly, we have before us a most notable and instructive example and illustration of the progress of the age.

But did it never occur to those who have been most forward by their proceedings to give to the world some memorable expression of their devotion to the cause of the equal rights of mankind, and of their abhorrence of all such despotic governments as that of Russia, that it was proper to consider whether the system of Russia, in the present condition of her population, may not be the very best that could be devised to advance their civilization and prepare them for ultimate freedom? Did it never occur to them to consider with what caustic severity the Czar of Russia might retort their criminations of his Government, and their pompous declaration in favor of liberty and equality, by a slight reference to our

www.ingramcontent.com/pod-product-compliance
Lightning Source LLC
LaVergne TN
LVHW020643110826
845149LV00004B/1339

* 9 7 8 1 4 1 8 1 9 0 3 2 3 *